To

From

Date

ISBN 978-1-4002-1001-5

Cover and Interior Illustration: Julianne St. Clair
Interior Design: Kait Lamphere

Printed in the United States

20 21 22 /LSC/ 5 4 3

PUMPKIN SPICE & EVERYTHING NICE

COLORING BOOK

Illustrated by Julianne St. Clair

HOW GRATEFUL AND THANKFUL

I am
to the *Lord*

because he is so good.

I will SING praise

to the name of the Lord

WHO IS ABOVE

all *lords.*

PSALM 7:17 TLB

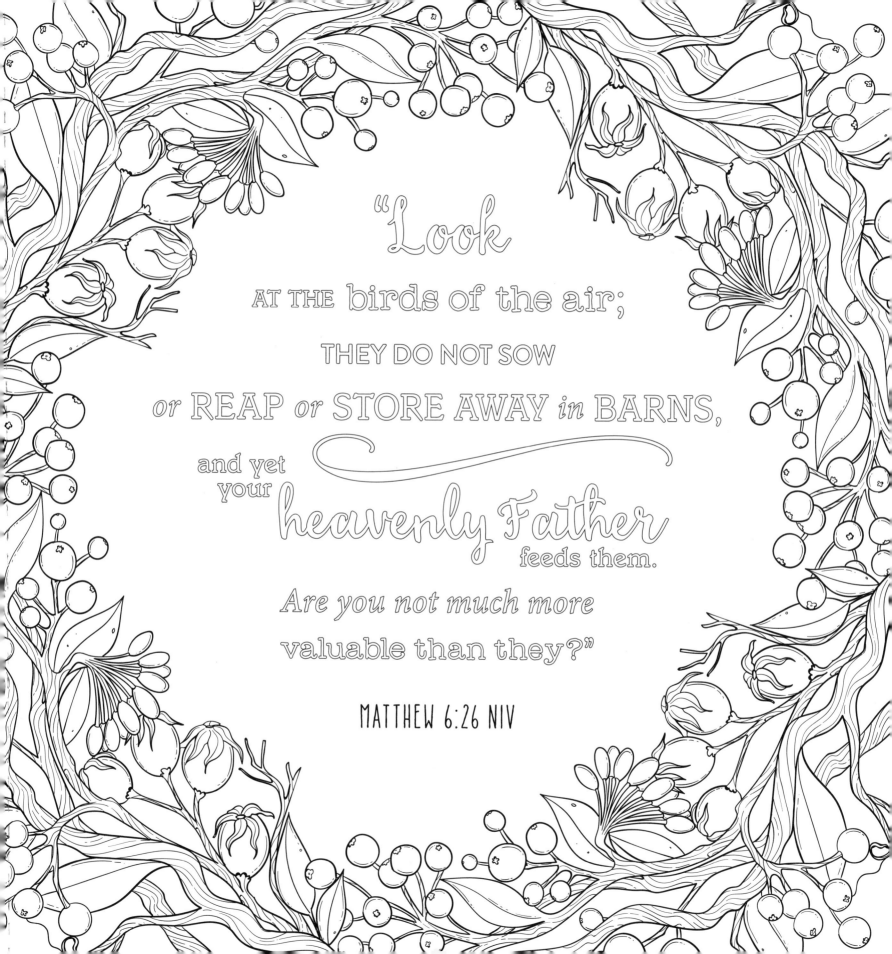

"Look AT THE birds of the air; THEY DO NOT SOW or REAP or STORE AWAY in BARNS, and yet your heavenly Father feeds them. Are you not much more valuable than they?"

MATTHEW 6:26 NIV

Autumn...
the YEAR'S LAST,
loveliest smile.

WILLIAM CULLEN BRYANT

O LORD our God, all this abundance that we have prepared to BUILD YOU A HOUSE for Your holy name, ... is from Your HAND, and is all Your own.

1 CHRONICLES 29:16

AUTUMN

is the mellower season,

AND

what WE lose

IN *flowers*

we more than gain

IN *fruits.*

SAMUEL BUTLER

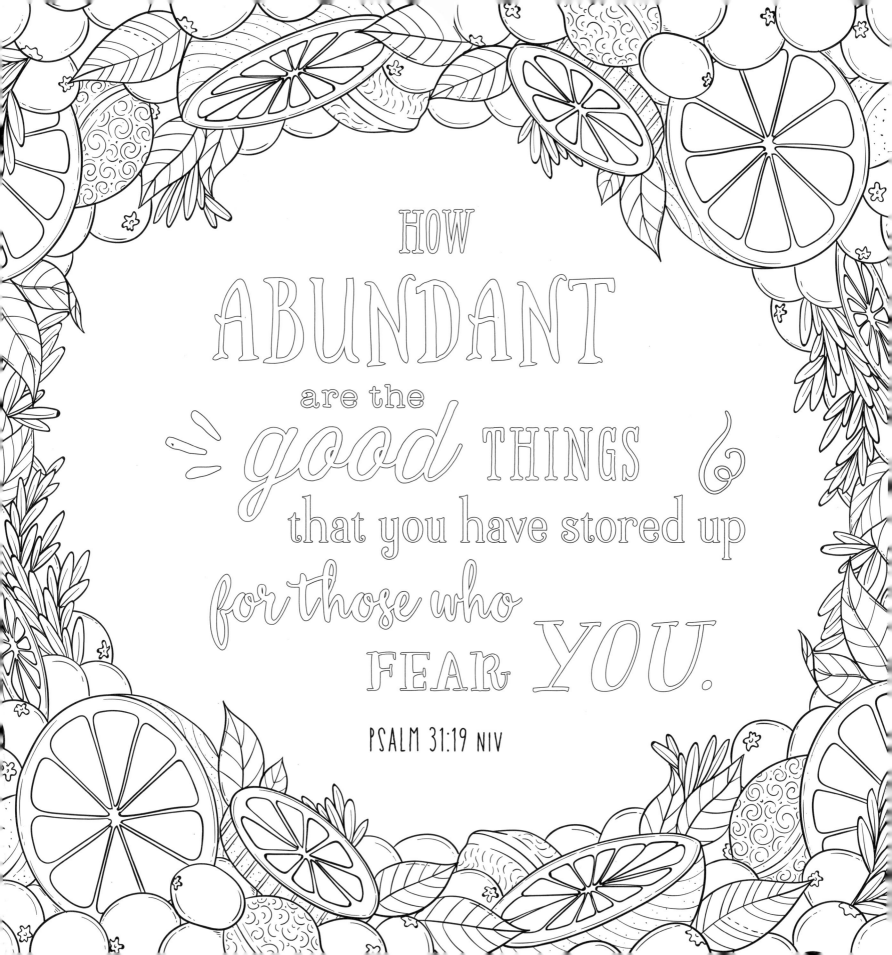

HOW
ABUNDANT
are the
good THINGS
that you have stored up
for those who
FEAR YOU.

PSALM 31:19 NIV

LET US

not

BECOME WEARY in DOING GOOD, for at the proper time WE WILL REAP a HARVEST if we DO NOT give up.

GALATIANS 6:9 NIV

My God shall SUPPLY ALL YOUR need according to his riches in GLORY by Christ Jesus.

PHILIPPIANS 4:19

Oh, HOW GREAT is Your goodness... WHICH YOU HAVE prepared for those who TRUST in You.

PSALM 31:19

Hoodies.
BONFIRES.
Cuddling.

Fall is here.

··· THIS ···

is the
day the LORD

HAS MADE;

We will *rejoice*

AND BE

GLAD

in it.

PSALM 118:24

Hayrides and pumpkin pies and golden SKIES

Oh, give thanks to THE LORD, FOR HE IS good!

For His mercy ENDURES forever.

1 CHRONICLES 16:34

NO SPRING NOR SUMMER
beauty HATH SUCH *grace*
·········· *as* I HAVE SEEN *in* ··········
ONE *autumnal* FACE.

JOHN DONNE

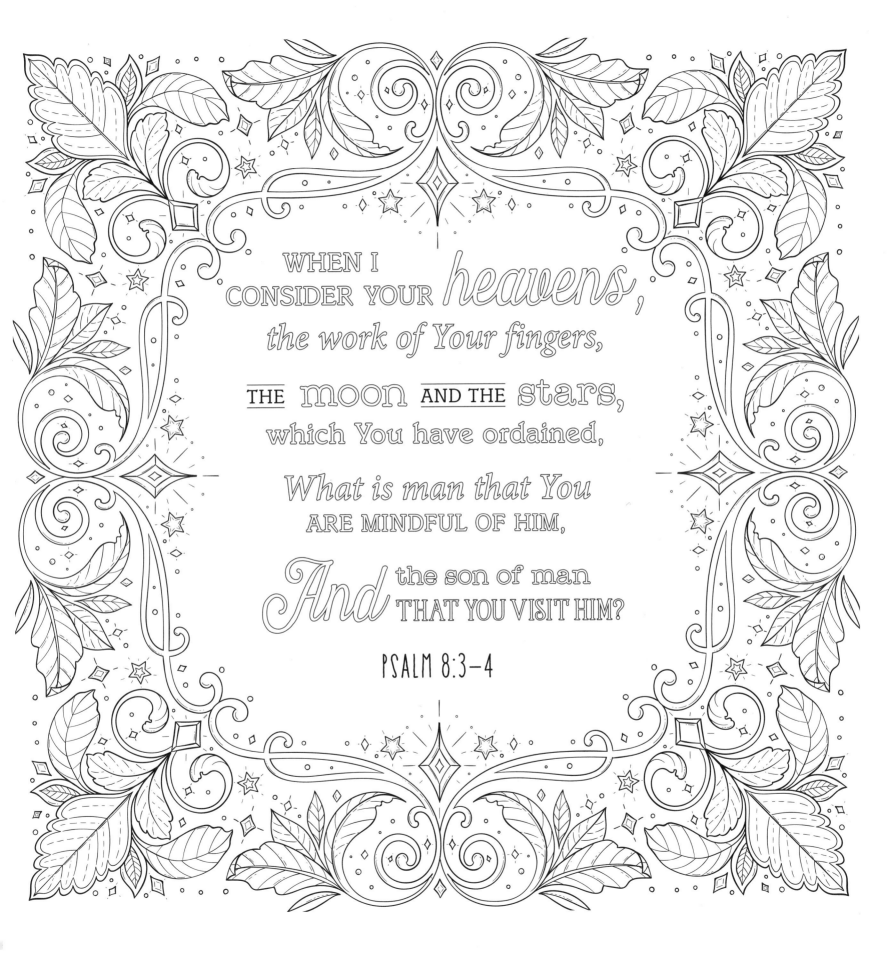

WHEN I CONSIDER YOUR *heavens,*
the work of Your fingers,
THE moon AND THE stars,
which You have ordained,
What is man that You
ARE MINDFUL OF HIM,
And the son of man
THAT YOU VISIT HIM?

PSALM 8:3–4

"As LONG as *the earth endures,* SEEDTIME and HARVEST, COLD and HEAT, ·············· SUMMER and WINTER, ··········DAY and NIGHT will NEVER cease."

GENESIS 8:22 NIV

Every LEAF
·····································
speaks bliss to me,
·····································
fluttering from
the
AUTUMN tree.

EMILY BRONTË

The EARTH
is THE LORD'S,
and all its fullness,
The world
& those who dwell
THEREIN.

PSALM 24:1

THE
heavens
declare THE GLORY *of God;*

THE *skies*

PROCLAIM *the work of*
HIS HANDS.

PSALM 19:1 NIV

BE patient, then, *brothers & sisters,* *until* THE LORD'S *coming.* SEE how the farmer waits for the LAND to yield its valuable crop, • • • • • *patiently waiting for* • • • • • *the* AUTUMN *and* SPRING *rains.* YOU too, be patient and stand firm, because the Lord's coming is *near.*

JAMES 5:7–8 NIV

THE
tints of
AUTUMN...
a mighty flower garden
BLOSSOMING *under the* SPELL
of the enchanter,
frost.

JOHN GREENLEAF WHITTIER

I will praise you, LORD, my God, with all my heart; I will glorify your name FOREVER

— Psalm 86:12 —

I'm so glad
I LIVE IN ······
a world
WHERE THERE ARE
OCTOBERS.

L. M. MONTGOMERY,
ANNE OF GREEN GABLES

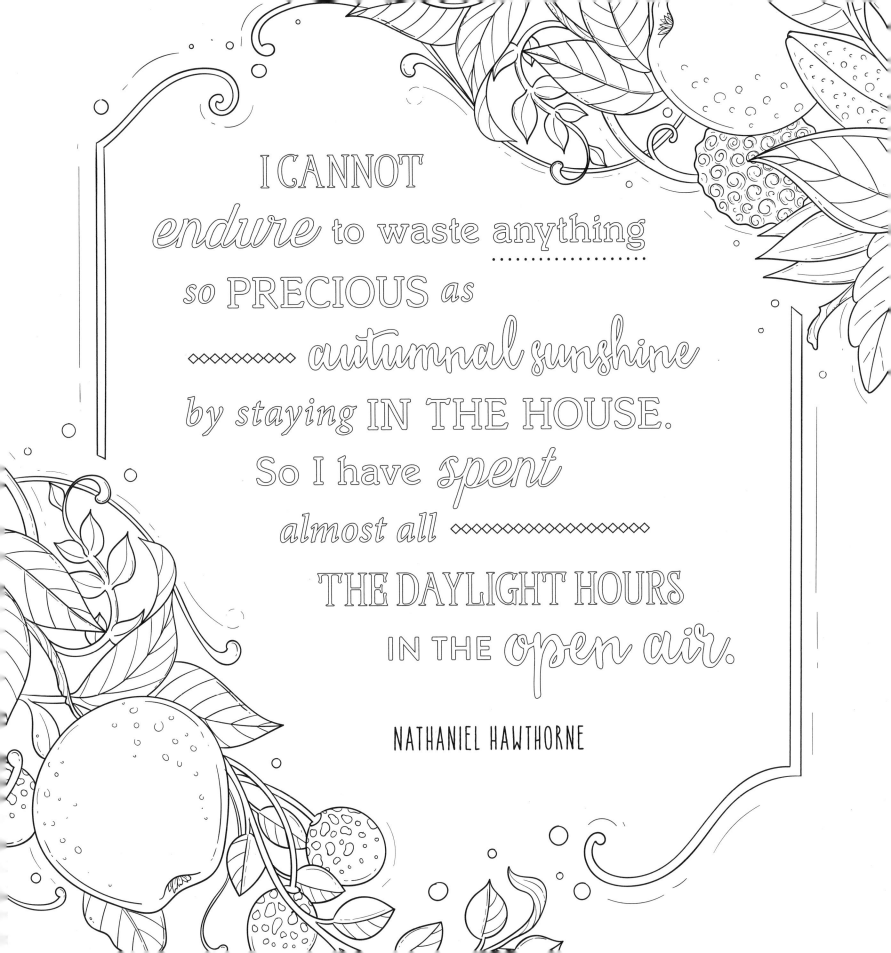

I CANNOT *endure* to waste anything so PRECIOUS as *autumnal sunshine* by staying IN THE HOUSE. So I have *spent* almost all THE DAYLIGHT HOURS IN THE *open air.*

NATHANIEL HAWTHORNE

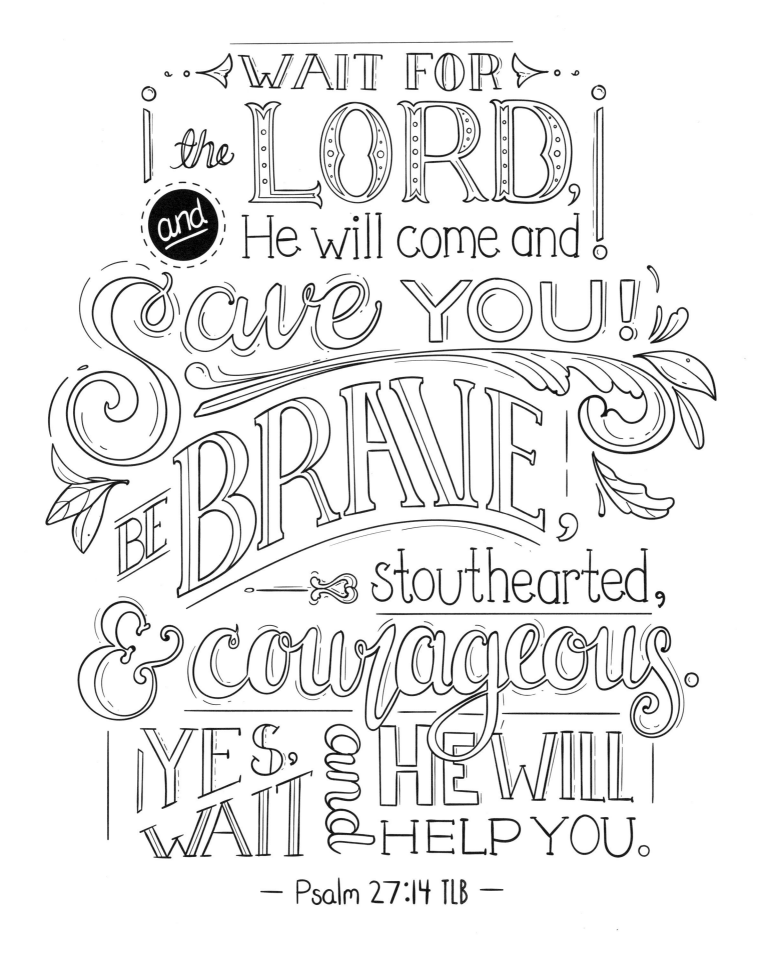

LET THE peace OF GOD RULE IN YOUR hearts AND BE thankful

Colossians 3:15

HOW *beautifully* LEAVES GROW OLD. HOW FULL OF *light* & *color* .... *are their* .... LAST DAYS.

JOHN BURROUGHS

Just
BEFORE
THE death of flowers,
. . . . . and BEFORE they
are buried in snow,
there comes a
festival season
when nature is all
aglow.

I WILL GIVE THANKS to YOU, LORD, with all my heart; I WILL TELL OF all your WONDERFUL deeds.

PSALM 9:1 NIV

Thou blossom *bright* WITH autumn dew, and COLORED
········· WITH THE ·········
heaven's own blue.

WILLIAM CULLEN BRYANT

WILD is the
·········· *music*
of AUTUMNAL WINDS
amongst the
faded WOODS.

WILLIAM WORDSWORTH

Light BREEZE, colorful LEAVES, BARE trees. It *must* be *autumn.*